The rhythms are ai matter that speaks of a real talent. You ought to be publishing.

— John Berryman, POET [1914-1972]
*(Excerpt from a personal letter
to Kath Howell, 1966)*

[Kath Howell's poems] are personal, unassuming, and witty. Perhaps my favorite was "Subtext for a Flowery Greeting"—but all these poems have subtexts, mutterings, asides. There's nothing quite like them.

— Malcolm Cowley, CRITIC [1898–1989]
(Quote from a personal letter, 1982)

At first, nothing much grabbed me. So I began again from the back and found many poems that delighted me. Some really world-class plays-on-words (and great internal rimes)... Made me think of William Bronk. Made me envious.

— Peter Kane Dufault, 2001
POET, *Looking in all Directions*

Kath sees the world in a convergence of kindness and truth, uncovering a latent goodness in people, places and times that is neither sentimental nor spiritually aloof. She's the neighbor at the window jotting down our common meanderings in a way that reveals their hidden holiness. Like C. S. Lewis, she takes joy seriously without losing its playfulness. In this way she is, like all true poets, a prophet as well...a voice for a larger Love.

— Michael Kelly Blanchard, 2002
SONGWRITER/MUSICIAN
Author, *Unsung Heroes*
Co–host, *There Is Love*, PBS Special

BRush
WITH
REALiTY

Kath Howell

Brush with Reality

POEMS AND DRAWINGS

BY KATH HOWELL

COLLEGE AVENUE PRESS
Clinton Corners, New York

BRUSH WITH REALITY: Poems and Drawings
by Kath Howell

Copyright © 2002 by Kathleen Howell

Cover art and design by the author, in collaboration with The Attic Studio and Corby Design. Back cover reflection on "Real Poetry" by Dana Gioia, courtesy of Mars Hill Audio, Charlottesville, VA, Vol. 51, July/August 2001.

COLLEGE AVENUE PRESS
is an imprint of
THE ATTIC STUDIO Publishing House
P.O. Box 75 • Clinton Corners, NY 12514
Phone: 845-266-8100 • Fax: 845-266-5515
E-mail: CollegeAvePress@aol.com

PRINTED IN THE UNITED STATES OF AMERICA
10 9 8 7 6 5 4 3 2 1   FIRST EDITION

Library of Congress Cataloging-in-Publication Data

Howell, Kath, 1940–
    Brush with reality : poems and drawings / by Kath Howell.
        p. cm.
    ISBN 1-883551-40-4 (alk. paper)
    I. Title.
PS3608.O955 B78 2002
811'.6—dc21

                                        2002009038

For my parents

JANE AND WILLIE HOWELL

Mom taught me to parse sentences, showing me
how words matter—especially in action: just hold
on to your hats, and press on, regardless.

When it dawned on me that I probably wouldn't
grow up to play shortstop for the Brooklyn Dodgers,
Dad showed me that growing up was worth it
anyway.

*The lines are fallen unto me
in pleasant places; yea, I
have a goodly heritage.*

— PSALM 16:6

CONTENTS

II. LITTLE FIGURES HERE AND THERE

V. IN MY BACKYARD

VI. THE EVENING *and the* MORNING
of the SAME DAY

VII. FRAGMENTS

FOREWORD

*B*ROWSE HERE as in a bookstore, or library. Listen as you might in a coffeehouse. Talking with friends, overhearing strangers and other background sounds, including music.

What's really said is between the lines—although local color spills outside them. Since the poems in this book have been selected from several sequences, and the illustrations from many sketchbooks, they represent a long time and a lot of space. Words and pictures work together on some pages, play against each other on another. Contrapuntal partners—like us.

Look at familiar views: social, political, religious, and geographic, as if you were among tourists. Speakers of strange languages making the best of it: sense and friends.

– I –

from

A YEAR AND A DAY

Traditionally, a fugitive
might go free
after a year and a day
in sanctuary.

LIFE IN THE REAL WORLD

Across the lawn
lights have been off and on all night.
The house next door is bright as Christmas,
more than light enough for me to watch the Smiths,
in keeping with the Joneses, give a reception
as clear in my living room
as on TV—

      A commercial interrupts

      Reality!

That's my door! Who knocks?
I unfumble several locks, stumble
stare. Always ready to lend a hand a cup of brandy,
a sleeping draught, a sugar substitute
I take great care lest some passing stranger
appearing desperate to use the phone—

Police!
An emergency?
Not exactly, Ma'am. A citizen's arrest
Cardiac. Surprised a burglar in his own home
and him a common fence
disguised as an electronic surveillance system.
But not to worry. All that can be, will be done.
The police go.
Ours is a vigilant community; we don't walk in fear.
We run.

SCATTERING THROUGH THE CITY

people run errands, walk dogs
sit and talk business
economical gossip that does no real harm
only clears the air.
Dirty linen hangs from every window
flags and banners flying
like laundry.

Naked but clean
people stroll home slowly
stuck in their skin
tight corners and worn-out curbs
dogged men and women

who did their best?
Who scrubbed the front steps
polished and shone the sky?
The rain washed these shabby streets.
and the sun lay down on the sidewalks
licking the shadows dry.

IF THE PEOPLE WHO LIVE HERE
LIKE IT

why is a lot left empty
in the midst of all this overcrowded space?
The buildings seem structurally sound

proof against burglars;
with only a wall between them
the neighbors lean out of windows to talk
hanging words in the air like laundry

underbodies worn and washed and dried so often
they are transparent as delicate curtains
Has nobody anything to hide?

The trashman says very little goes to waste;
things are used until they fall apart.
Only the lives led in these solid houses
are thrown away.

ACTUALLY IN AMERICA
THERE ARE STILL SOME TOWNS

where people paint their fences white
and worry about what to wear on Sunday

not that it matters much
since anything goes in church,
even people

who prey quietly,
stripping houses
taking TVs, radios, tape decks, record players

forgiven as thieves for making the image work,
the kids who deliver the Sunday papers
can't help notice how nobody's home

helping the next-door neighbor
hood
fence.

GOING SOMEWHERE

this small town acquired
city streets

straight across backyards
between fences; they broke trees
and laid the forests down
framing houses now abandoned

along the edge of town.

And there are no green fields left
behind—

tall shadows, only building blocks
one on top another
trying to touch the sky
leaving no room for roofs

little attic windows peak through broken shutters
holding the heavens up
watching the world go by.

THERE IS ALWAYS THAT FACE
IN THE UPSTAIRS WINDOW

Maybe that unwanted child again
with no better place to go, staring
leaning against the pain
pressed to the glass, crying:

> Throw stones! Throw stones!
> Break my window box
> my bones and skin, somebody
> let me out
>
> or please come in.

AFTER JURY DUTY

The long slow jumble of honest men
shakes hands, the judge waves back
dismissing all differences between right and wrong

letting the fellowship of peers adjourn
to homely gray areas between black and white
watching the evening news

they switch off their own judgement
and count the cost of living
death, taxes
war, peace
football

heroes who are really important
whether the police protect them or not.

GLORIA MUNDY AT HOME

The old lady working at her box
looks out for herself in the window.
Neither longing nor lonely, she knows not where time went
nor where it goes; only that it will return
familiar. Too often faced
this self in the mirror pales,
faint by comparison, faded beyond fond memory.
Only an image remains
reversed
returning

inward upon itself, at last first.
The old lady tends her planting.
Weeds, fertilizes, reseeds,
reliant upon purified water and air
conditioned
reflexes twitch long after death.
Dying is instantaneous; life lingers on.

ELLA AMBUTT

Neat, tidy mother of two sons
fathered by a union organizer
back in the days when there was work
right after the war
her husband died, leaving her
next to nothing
so she worked nights
wondering if there were war now
would the boys have something to do
other than stay home
picking fights?

MISS PALTRY AND MISS WEIN

Two shabby lace handkerchiefs
yellowed, fluttery
wrinkled as faces
wave to each other. Tears
dry in the breeze.
Had they but loved!
But love in those days (as now)
came between two people
no matter how.

BOWED BARBARA

Born poor
she never got enough of nothing
but what she snatched or grabbed. At free lunch
she took twice what she needed
saving some for supper
wrapped in her apron around the fat.
double coupon days, she clipped good as Got-rocks
proving there's nothing beyond redemption.

INSULL AMBUTT

Never left home except once
for war; never knew (nor cared)
what he was fighting for.
Death in distant lands
showed him all the world has to offer:
killing and blood, like home.
Guns and knives spoke no strange language;
he understood enemies as well as friends
and never wonders why nobody won or lost
the war that never ends.

GRACE

Poor lorn wellfaring stranger
her gripped the shelf
same label; one jar after another
shocked, stocked still
unable to match her diet to the avowed ingredients,
her unfathomable body chemistry defied coupons
clipped for special savings.
Grace hungered for more than bread alone.
Eating raw catfood by herself
she dreamed of fish, cooked on a forked stick
over an open fire
she never smelled nothing
burning
not even herself.

ADDIE RINKLE

repeated the kind old words:

Day's ease, dear.

Let long slow hours keep company
awake, asleep; the subject's love
the form, familiar human.
Here's the place. The time
alas, is now. What happened?

Wonder why, not how.

VIRGIL STOUT WATCHES NEW SNOW

The little hours of evening
like twilight flicker
on houses locked in love
or prayer. Sound's a-sleeping
still somewhere
faint candles fill
dark's open window wide,
spill sparks outside. Light
falls quicker than night,
bright covers grounds, keeping
quiet wrapped in white.

THE LADY IN THE RED COAT

The lady in her red coat bravely crosses the bridge
stepping brightly into the wind
touching the rail lightly, she steps over the snow
drifts and slides, sides
slipping
tripping, she catches herself.
But the red hat, hiding her hair
blows away—bluegrey as the sky
flyaway, fly! Lady bugged eye
she watches out for mad children, dangerous as dogs.
She whooped and warcried long before they were born,
long before everybody she knew died,
forgotten, one by one. She lives
alone; nobody knows
she carries a gun.

THE BOMB WARDEN

Retired
honored for a life of useful service
he sit home, time on his hands
long and short like a clock, watching
work—work—work
daily he hate the sound of ticking
tock...tock...tock...
Destruction a device
intricate as a man's heart
beating, racing against, running
outstretched, twined as his hands,
the left and the right working
together
against time. He hate the ticking
so he collects broken clocks and watches
nobody wants (he gets them free,
a fortunate hobby for his slender pension).
Him, he sit home
dusting the carven figures
the vines and gardens, the springs
the gears forever fixed
frozen eternally, unwound
he flap he winging arms
singing
cuckoo! Cuckoo!

14

HILDE WALTHER

Her body bagged
skinsacks of wrinkled leather
pouched, drawn
lips pursed over the little used language of her youth
(grunts, screams
the argot of camps and transport)
she mouthed and numbered barracks,
barbs and wire. Remembering
exiles with only each other in common
she wept, waving neighbor kids off to camp.

GARY AMBUTT

Legged home from war with one less,
game and a glass eye as bright as his good one.
Blind to what he'd left behind
he waits for work like he was normal
missing nothing but the bus.
He's easily tricked when treated like regular people
so he plays dumb as an animal
dressed up human
like every other hero.

JERMAYNE JONSON

earns her living proofreading religious tracts;
letter by the spirit pervades her:
Credo! Credo!
says Jermayne Jonson of Argosy Prayers.
Go ahead: whisper. Nobody cares.

Gloved, booted,
fetching, but in no wise vain
glorious, she lives after work
learning to trade. Giving no quarter
and asking for change,
she hands old ladies over puddles
puts nickels in expired parking meters
returns abandoned shopping carts.

A sallow little saint,
believing as best she can, she's been mugged, raped,
martyred—but her bent old body hauls herself upstairs
halo and all, to glow in the dark of dreamless sleep.
When the wings of angels whir
fanning flames in winter, cooling the summer wind,
she's so grateful, Jermayne is
that she pets them bats. Blind? Crazy?
Says she's human
kind.

GAYLORD ENDERS, LIBRARIAN

Unjudged by covers
booklovers laugh and weep
imagining themselves heroes behind closed doors.
Due, overdue—
I renew tastes and peccadilloes,
read how-to between the lines. Dully, dry
stuck in the mud? Readers, rejoice!
Life circulates through open stacks
like blood.

SUBTEXT FOR A FLOWERY GREETING

It's been ages, Myrtle
                    (Violet, Heather, Rose,
Boxwood, Thistle, Thorn…?) never called
you old so-and-so

and sew, sprigg'd lavender and thyme
passed all too fast; so quickly stitched
buttoned, hooked, eyed
                    (with everybody watching
it is hard to be natural, hard to believe
hours have been only minutes,
minutes no more than seconds) hands
                                   hold
                                   it, has been
how long? Reaping the sewn seams
pick'd, pluck'd threads
raised like eyebrows, amazed—
did no one know one so
so long
ago?

FRIENDS OF A LIFETIME

From feathered nests as brushed for Sunday
as soft felt hats
the little old ladies, joyful and poor
spoon whipped cream over coffee
and imagine syrup, and donuts, and cake.

Sweet toothless wonders! Clutching, cackling,
curbing furry and imagined pets,
clapping their worn white gloves
over hands clean as their own

spruced up after a lifetime of dirtywork,
they scrub their porches still
and invite each other over to rest,
as worried as they ever were
counting on habits as fixed as their incomes

they know the world will still go round
no matter how many old friends
sleep still and tidy
underground.

EARLY SNOW

barely covers the ground, only a light frost
on earth already cold
chills the lawn. Carefully
so as not to damage the grass
a woman rakes. Lean as the wind
she blows into her hands
rattling finger bones like dry, pressed leaves.
She looks at her house
standing thinly dressed in white
and very old.

FATHER WIGHTY

Turn the glass ball over.
A shower of plastic snow whirls round the little scene
whitening the roof of the woodcutter's hut
covering fenceposts. Gray deer
nuzzle pines at the edge of the forest
hidden 'til the storm is over
and the liquesphere clear as a midsummer's day.

Away in the distance
a tiny train, pulled by a string of smoke
moves through the view,
passing fields of carved cows, a bridge, a river,
a painted town churched
steepled, peopled with a cutout cardboard crowd.

Here is a world we have lost
as surely as triptychs and ornamented books;
as surely as the foreshortened paradise
circled by saints; as surely as
the sun no longer revolves around the earth
we have lost something like faith, along with a world
we could hold in our hands.

LITTLE, IF WE KNOW,
HAS HARDLY LESSENED CARE

Carrying her basket of eggs and sufferings
candles and candles
the goodhearted girl sets forth

clutching coals for Grandma,
a spark of fire to warm black pot and black kettle
enflaming the gossip that crackles the hearth.

She speaks to no one in the woods
knowing better. But, scared by a strange animal,
she trips—

trees burn.
In the blackened forest
shadowing their former selves,
brave girl and Grandma enjoy roast wolf
(their first full meal in weeks)
wishing only

bigger teeth
to crack the tough white bones.

GLORIA MUNDY'S BAD END

She lunched in town, ate
late, alone, went home
grown into the shadow of herself.
Something shone. A muddy star
silver in the puddled street!
Light fingered as a pocket, picked
clean, her last cent
spent, weary, she meant no harm;
shrank from suffering
small as a child. Huddled
in the roadbed, cuddled
a mugger took her life.
She hadn't anything else
worth keeping alive
or dead.

THE DECEASED IS SURVIVED
BY HIS WIFE, RESIDING

in a small apartment over the grocery
smelling of fruity vegetables and frozen meat
she got out of bed
rock-bottom reality, sleeping the long sleep
the preacher said (but she knew better
after the wake)

up early in the morning
hung over the counter
costs rising
high overhead, she stretched
her long neck lean as a dollar
her face shucked in the mirror marked meats and poultry

she opened the store as usual:
carried yesterday's papers down cellar for the cat,
reduced the prices on day-old goods,
cleared the community bulletin board of used notices
(Garage Sale...Old Clothes...TV, Almost New...)

and threw a bucket of coleslaw on the floor
and waited quietly
for the first customer
to slip.

LIKE ANY OTHER CREATURE

a habit's comfort. A same old thing
kept secret, close; second to none but nature
calling for helping hand to mouth
(to muffle cough and sneeze, nips
the milky fingertips)—A terrible shriek in the night!
Lights shine in the bright corner…scuffling,
scrambling…
whatever beast came shambling through these shadows
won't be hiding here again.

ALMOST QUIET

Soundly
some small houses sleep
since the next-door neighbor guards
the common yards, and walls that watch the windows
hide the street
turning every corner
crossing at the light
respectable village shadows
bid themselves good-night.

LONG NIGHT LOOKS
TOWARDS MORNING

in darkness dying, like the lady down the hall.
Today her chill, as something still
and gray slips
but not away.

LULLABY

The aged grin and cackle
baring secrets behind a withered mask
but uncaring attendants, who hear little
and listen for less, turn away
embarrassed by incontinent ideas
as they have not been
by wrinkled bodies in the bath.
But frail old voices insist;
stage whispers rise, rumbling like steam
hissing and heating the pipes
bubbling over—

> What do we know and why
> will no one ever ask?

Remember, remember…that's what we want to do.
Not string beads, nor sing, nor stretch
these stringy old muscles. Let us look back
see how far we've come.
We want to show you, tell you,
help you on your way, for you'll make this journey, too
some day. Keep us company; we've no one else.
We've only a little while
with such a long way to go —

> What do we know and why
> will no one ever ask?

But puzzles and crafts and cards are what's offered
to keep their minds off other things 'til lunch;
then it's rest from one to three, eat early dinner,
watch TV. No wonder they nod and doze!
Reliving a lifetime is hard work
moonlighting, making ends meet
leaves little time for introductions,
polo, bridge, outrageous parties.
The aged sigh, and suck their gums.
They've been there and back; they know
the Kingdom comes—

What do we know and why
will no one ever ask?

NEEDS MET

by strangers, barely introduced
before performing intimate ministrations
with mechanical dispatch: filling bellies
like forms, staunching blood,
binding wounds, cutting red tape
spilled

all over the ground
into dust, gutted
decent privacy is laid to rest
shivering in Sunday best
shrugged over shreds of dignity
worn out

in this cold
shoulder to shoulder, survivors stand
outlawed, outnumbered, outspoken
lost souls found, at last
under stones unturned
uncast.

DREAMING IN SIGN LANGUAGE

Her hands moved
holding, shaping, feeling
fingering the fine threads of meaning

weaving and winding, unwinding
her hands talk to each other
too tired to do anything but open up,

they let go.

KATIE BUMP

survived by a long illness
and her few close friends
laid rest the body
she loved best. A farmwife
married to the land
she slept beneath a stone inscribed
before she died:

> She loved her neighbors
> and was kind to animals as well
> but what the difference was
> she'd never tell.

OLD ANIMAL

Is this, o self, my same
the I my body's been
and sheltered by? None other
name, the now familiar

came—a stout companion,
soul tucked me in
side myself
maidservant, skin.

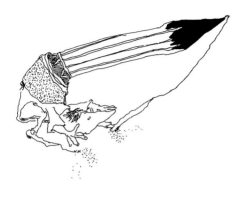

– II –

from

Li TTLE FiGURES HERE AND THERE

They paint in Flanders only to deceive
the external eye, things that gladden you
and of which you cannot speak ill.
Their painting is of stuffs, bricks and mortar,
the grass of the fields, the shadows of trees,
and bridges and rivers, which they call landscapes,
and little figures here and there.

— MICHELANGELO

SOME OF THE POEMS
IN THIS SECTION
ARE FROM

CASTING the MIRACLES

...not bread upon the waters, but a section
of a mystery cycle, creation and fall, with
reference to life outside the Garden.

— and —

UNDER the FIG TREE

...where greater things than these are seen.

FALL

Knowing of cold, loneliness and guilt
nothing but each other, Adam and Eve
clothed in their new nakedness
went into the wilderness. Green
as the garden they'd left, ripening
ready for harvest

and fall.

IT WAS ALL SO NEW TO THEM

after the garden: love, travail,
finding themselves father and mother.
Once Adam and Eve brought forth Cain
they made him a brother, planning
for the first time, far
in the future they said:
when whatever happens
happens to us
the boys will have each other.

BACK TO BASICS

The lowest common denominator
divides, conquers
reduces everything to its own level.
Watered down, diluted
tomorrow will be
one of the days of the week
no matter what the strong try to do about it.

SCHOOL CLOTHES

New or handed down
a little big,
bought to be grown into
like the mind, or out of
like the body.

ARTS

Without its image, would reality be
recorded, lettered and numbered?
Not everything that measures up
must be written down. Dances
leap to mind. Felt in the flesh
bones rattle, blood stirs. Embodied
souls take heart, and form. Familiar
shapes step lively, lithe and warm.

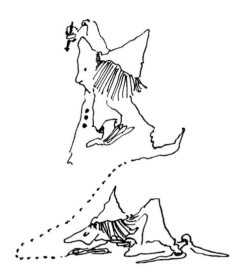

MULTIPLE AS CHOICE

right answers proliferate.
Visions are qualified,
clouded. Nothing's simple,
neither questions nor explanations.
Filled in, blanks no longer exist.
True or false?

WORD PLAY

interlocks. Spells
standing one upon another
sway. Letters lean,
teeter. The tower tumbles.
Crumbles. Chipped,
the old alphabet rebuilds
Babel, of writers' blocks.

PHONICS

Syllable by syllable
the sounds of sounding out
soften the hardest words.

BOOK LEARNING

Linear, sequential
page after page, book upon book
shelved, stacked, sheer volume sustains
length, breadth and depth:
all the dimensions of life.

GRAMMAR

Nouns gnash their teeth,
verbs hush. Justified by rules,
exceptions prove unruly.
Subjects object. Parsed,
pushed beyond the common parlance
words mean too much.
Like people.

MAGNETIC PROPERTIES

Opposites attract.
Coldhearted metallic bits cling to each other
through thick and thin; like repels like.
Unlikely antagonists fight
tooth and claw, attacking the self
same enemy. Nothing's natural in law.

ECONOMICS

The world turns
on a dime. Brother,
can you spare me
a penny for your thoughts?
Talk is cheap, but advice is cheaper—
to get something for nothing
give no quarter
and ask for change.

POLITICAL SCIENCE

Stopping for whistles
races are run in fits and starts.
Rings, hats and platforms scattered
across the country litter the landscape
with broken dreams, rules and promises.
Elections are held to determine
who cleans up, after all the messy parties.

IN THIS WORLD
THAT STRUGGLES ON

like people
all alone in space
stars shine
so far away
shadows stay safe
all night, blinded
by light.

EDGING THE SAINTS' TALES

scraps of landscape linking one to another
twist and curl, like a serpent
slinking away past pilgrim's details
bordering the real with this remembered house,
holding that hill, those trees, these roots
wrapped around stony ground
under flowered banks of a stream
running, running. Quite close to home
made-up, typical, familiar faces beam
as if recognition were just around the corner
cutting away a roof, a wall
a window, watching. Watching
a virgin Eve reach for silken fruit,
her farmer turns away. An enamelled jewelbug nests
in the gnarl of a leafy bush. Strangely,
for all the sun, there's no shade.
Dogs lie in the brightness;
their fur gleams with so much brushing
even the paint is shiny. Strangely,
such colors never fade.

KINGDOM EVERALL I

Unable to speak (and her cries
were far from music) she drew
conclusions, lining the shadows like clouds
covering abysmal darkness
with scratches. Below the surface,
bloody bones. Skinned deep
she knew her own way was home
making believe in something
even herself.

GOLD MEDAL

When a dream comes true, reality
leaps into another dimension

that of the spirit, shaped
lean, athletic

graceful as a body.

WHEN WORDS WERE YOUNG

It was an older language then
and clear, shrill as a child's horning
warning of want or fear, told and tasted
on the tongue. Mean or magical
meanings were original,
beginnings new, and endings
still sharp and unexpected stung
not just the ear. Heard
without a word, for instance: "love."
And love, as to a hand outstretched,
drew near.

PANTOMIME FOR A WINTER DAY

Shadows fur, bearded with breath
mist rises from solid streams,
smokes, steams. There's no fire
but cold burns

warming the animal kingdom
where beasts reborn beyond temptations
leap and play. Pure in the snow
men and women stumble and run

stretch thin, twigged arms
toward each other, unable to reach
they hold their own;
cold is all that matters.
Without it, they would melt away.

ONCE UPON THE ELEMENTAL

light and dark, it was earth's turning
dialed the sun
burning a both-ended candle
while sands were ground into glass.
Times pass the time

and clock the race, run fast
past time's familiar face. Hands
clasped in a round of time and space
surround bright painted figures, dance
and ring. Chimes tinkle; symbols clash
or sing; signs interlock —

o those were legendary times
and past-times, made to outlast
the present! Tense, the anxious
future's cast: efficient
unencumbered. Digital,
time is numbered.

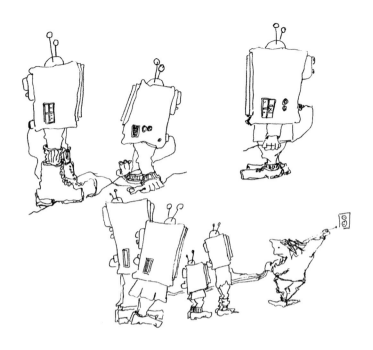

CHILDREN'S GAMES, AFTER BREUGHEL

Way after. Things have changed: just imagine, unjust
pretend.
Little boys stick-em-up, shooting live bullets;
little girls push doll carriages, with live babies inside.
Miniature Mother Hoods and Father Hoods,
all the little Hoods abuse each other,
affording the barren necessities of drugs
alcohol and video addiction. Creatures of habit
breaking rules, making believe
this is all there is to growing up:

> play for real
> feelings and things
> break
> even in fun.

LIKE WITCHES, THE PROFESSIONS HAVE THEIR FAMILIARS

Scribes forage among words: conversant with jargon
they translate the vernacular into the incomprehensible
because there are meanings in plain language
nobody wants to understand. So the unsayable remains
unsaid; who wants to talk about the living
dead? Familiar and homey as violence in the streets
societal dysfunctions subvert, tempt, bedevil.
The law–abiding have been locked up;
the same, straitjacketed by rites that went wrong;
values, clarified, are added, taxed. Still
but unstill, our ancient world of daily rounds
turns as the earth does, circling the sun
light shines, and darkness follows.

BEASTS OF OUR BURDENS

bodies, bearing the souls'
searching for something
besides the self
serving the uncertain. Still
loyal bundles of aches and pains
age into accepting this
last untimely business
lying quiet, as if at peace,
and dumb. They can't call us
yet we come, curled tight
against the cold, or cooling
stretched in sunmade shade.
Tame and untame animals
close eyes, asleep, vulnerable
even in our wildest dreams.

TAMING THE WILD

forest to field, animals trampled the bush;
beasts grazed grasslands down to the nubble,
pawed dirt, gnawed the feeding hands

mounting old commands: Sit! Stay!
Heel! Whoa! Gee-up! Mush! Kneel!
Roll over and play

not dead, just kidding. The old trick:
don't kick the flank, or yank the reins,
the leash, the yoke; use carrot, stick.

Simple folktales pulled
no punches, turning the herd
with a single word: naming the child.

KINGDOM EVERALL II

clothes the line
dresses the turkey and salad
while kids scream
with laughter. She leaves them

in stitches, hemmed, hawed.
Grown out of her skin
deep roots, she questions doubts
sure some things are certain.

Belief brushes her sleeve like snow,
each flake unique and beautiful,
blessed (although with less
than mortal span). From such crystals comes
the avalanche, whitening
the wicked works of man.

BECAUSE THE FRIENDLY POEM

Came, warm
and fuzzy, before it was
even called, I wasn't quite
ready. It pushed and nuzzled
hungry to be loved
so I fed it
what I had at hand
holding my breath
it grew, shaped, changed
my life, too. Known
if not by name
to keep each other close
and safe from harm, claws sheathed
we snuggled
arm in arm.

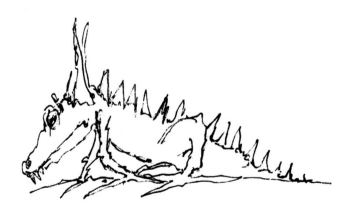

THERE IS NO JUSTICE

blind as faith
leaping like little hills
into a wordly wilderness, all flowered
field and trees.In this landscape of temptations
all fruits please. Not since Paradise
have old masters painted
such scenes as these: gold leaves
that glitter in the forest
covering, for one bright moment, Adam
and his Eve's delight.

Give up this world? It's hardly mine
to part with! Unvarnished, colors fade;
gilt, tarnished, turns to rust; flakes crimp and dwindle
into dust. From this God made not only world
but me. Get thee behind, blackhooded renunciate!
Undone by light, shade pales, dark fails.
Blind, bedazzled, shadow follows substance.
Run after the sun.

SKETCH

Shadows line
a piece of scrap paper
where it was crumbled

wrinkled like a face

masking the blank look
of an empty page.

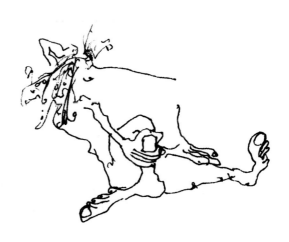

COLOR GALLERY

WHAT ISN'T BLACK OR WHITE
ISN'T NECESSARILY GRAY

KINSHIP

BEACHED, WITHOUTEN TOWEL

SPRING IS NOT JUST FOR CLEANING

RAGGED SAILORS
AT A YARD SALE

52

GETTING INTO SHAPE BY STRETCHING
THE IMAGINATION
BEYOND BELIEF....

WINDOWS. BOXED

FALL

" FOR EVERY TREE IS KNOWN
BY HIS OWN FRUIT..."
LUKE 6:44

STAINED GLASSES

WALK... AND LET THE COLORS RUN

COLOR GALLERY

– IV –

from

FIELD GUIDE TO WORDS

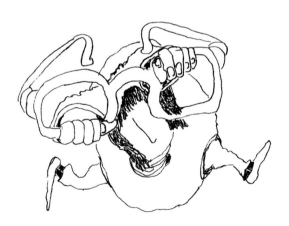

THE LIFE OF THE POET

Illustrated by her poems

between the line
drawings, words
pencilled in the margins

picturing details
between birth and death,
illuminating the simplest things
embellishing events with fantastical decorations

gold leaf branching out
shinybright, a forest
shimmering like Christmas

trees
grown, stumped, pulped
for paper

work. The poet recycles
her life.

OLD ENOUGH TO READ

a theatre program,
to distinguish between cast and characters
but not understand the part
words play; to mouth the menu
slurping soupday; to follow the church service
the sequence of words waiting upon words
as handmaidens and harbingers pray

nosegay and boxlunch
gruntled and in merry pin
hie usward, eluding common parlance
circle, surrounding some special occasion

mysterious, liturgical words
lend a grace and beauty to life
meaning alone can never quite contain.
Much less express.

Anyone old enough to read has a right to know
the revised version may be clearer
but not necessarily more clearly understood.

ON THE OTHER SIDE OF THE FENCE

THE LANDSCAPE IS LITTERED
WITH SIGNS AND WONDERS

as spring spreads over the earth
in gay profusion, smells color and shape
delicate drawings

lining the landscape of language
itself. Hilly lumps of adjectives
cover clear outlines of nouns;
agile adverbs o'erleap crannied nooks
in pursuit of verbs
skimming mottled water
dancing on every surface
or sinking, settling down
grave and deliberate as a sluggish but still
moving tide rises conjunctively
clumped and clinging with barnacled grip.

All the world is words
well-chosen or not; names
given and taken, held in remembrance
when nothing but meaning is left
even after the landscape has fallen away
we will talk of ruins
left to the imagination.

MEDITATION IN
PREPARATION FOR PENTECOST

To have had few books
and those precious: handcopies
jewelled, illuminated
and clasped with gold

or clumsily printed
on rough paper, weatherstained
smudged, worn with reading
passed from hand to hand—

held dear, the written word was cherished
honored as the heir of the unwritten
translated into tongues
from whatever language the heart
spoke in the beginning.

REFERENCE ROOM

Homeless illiterates haunt the public library
wintering; wondering what is between the lines
so worth keeping warm and dry.
Catalogued along with seekers after light
they hanker after heat
huddle and sigh
not even asking a question
the librarian can't answer
why?

NOT WITH PEACE

The sword cuts
everything down to size;
put in perspective, the scale is
human. He meant what He said
running the vendors out of the temple
overturning the moneylenders table
returning unto Caesar his coins

withering the fig tree
driven to rage by unutterable spectres of indifference
and damnation, all that eternal agony.
So much suffering
and His own lying just ahead.

BIKERS ON A LEISURELY WORLD TOUR

The seasons cycle across the natural landscape
leaving manmade places behind, landmarking
the way back. Castles and cathedrals
and sites of lesser known local powers; stores,
filling stations, office buildings and banks
keep the crossroads company, left
along the way

bones of the dead
and the bodies of those living who stay behind
leave nothing to the imagination
not even themselves. Seasons recycle:
it's second nature, handsewn, hemstitched
womanmaid to serve and use along the way
the cloth and clay essentials of everyday.

SPRING'S A FEVER

Sweating out the last strains of flu
watching the geese fly north for
the season
searching streambeds and lakesides
waddling along beaches —

sand from the cold deep snows
blows everywhere. O dust! Thou art
gritty underfoot until the rains
wet and soften, squishy as clay

my kitchen floor is muddy enough to plant.
My lawn is sprouting thawed plastic bags
blown from everywhere but not back
across the street, weeds have begun to green.

The daffodils are here from the Cancer Society,
yellow as sun
shining all over the house;
Easter seals commemorate crippling diseases
especially those suffered by little children;
who knows what will strike next?
Even baseball—

what a wonder still is hope
springing eternal
this time of year.

NOT FOR NOTHING HAVE
WE NUMBERED OUR DAYS

Social security, telephone, license
lottery, credit —
we've got a lot to count on:
not just our fingers
but kept as close at hand.

CERTAINLY NO SIMPLE WORLD
SUSTAINS US HERE

Hard work makes wonders all her own
and seldom celebrates that sturdy craftsmanship
not done to last, but done to do again.
Daily, routines of cleaning
cooking, washing, ironing what will soon wrinkle
weeding, shopping (hauling heavy brown bags
groceries in, garbage out), mending, mowing
loving what is bound to grow up and go away
waiting, wondering
if this isn't worth it
what is?

ON A DAY AS BEAUTIFUL AS THIS

it is hard to worry about anything;
even poetry takes care of itself.
While working and nonworking mothers exchange jobs
househusbands, married to their work
raise roofs and expectations. Doing their best
as well as anybody, teachers teach,
farmers farm, doctors make housecalls
healing each other if not themselves. Children play
grownup: consumers and providers parenting
personhood. Pro-choice and Right-to-lifers
realize what they have in common: each other;
gangs of teenagers roam the streets, picking up litter;
we all hang on to the assembly line
drawn to each other as in a picture. Indeed
God's world could not be more perfect
had we made it ourselves!

ICE MELTS IN THE SUN
STILL WATERY
COLORS RUN AND GRAY
SHADOWS COOL
THE DAY

SHE LOVED

driving around
looking at landscapes,
and her sketches were beautiful:
accurate, evocative
temptations to paint

but the paintings were never finished.
There was always something else to do:
laundry, cooking, cleaning
the kids — and once they were grown
grandchildren, and her husband
sickening into a sort of second childhood
without the fun of a future.

He left her
a little something and some time to herself
but by then the landscape had changed;
her favorite view was still there
but in order to see it
she had to drive a little farther
climb a little higher, look a little longer
and see a little less. Getting home again
got harder and harder

but she kept going
even though that left her no strength to sketch
much less paint, so she sat back
closed her eyes
and looked at all the landscapes she had ever seen
and some she hadn't
remembered

for a long time.

ON NOT TAKING IT WITH YOU

Packing and repacking, worrying about what will wash
wrinkle and what can be worn twice
without anybody noticing

something important is always left behind
waving good-bye, and going
back

and forth, coming
home, Returning to well-remembered Zion

for this greatest journey
nothing is needed. Travel light
years away

leaving here
after. Life
is what is
used along the way.

WATER COLORS

Sea
shorelines
drawn along the water's edge
ripple; run together
tide pools puddle
mud dries as dust
darkens everything
cloud covers
    burst. Rainwashed
        away, all colors
           gray.

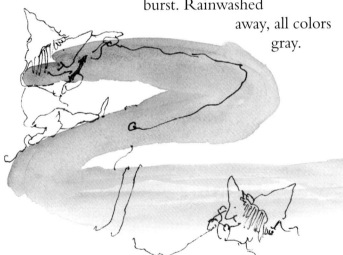

COVENANT

Passing her prime like a meridian
all flags flying and sails set
to catch what the wind blew, fair or fowl

old Granny Noah clambers on deck again
waiting on rain which God promised
and, since her husband believed
she, against all better judgement
left a house on high ground
going below with a bunch of animals.

"Dumb! That's what I were then
but lucky Grandpa weren't
or we'd none of us be here today,"
she tells her grandchildren
any young enough to gather round
as if they hadn't heard
and the few who sensed something
in the story beyond retelling
nestled close as if on Ararat.
Jane's kitten at the hug, Clarinda's pig
and Michael's furry dog — "Bless 'em!
Some you just can't separate," says Mrs. Noah
stepping over tracks across the floor
the muddy hair not dried to dust.
"Can always sweep clean," she hums
and bumbles, remembering
when that weren't good enough
and God washed the whole world down.

"Why, He even drowned my friends!" she cries
remembering the waved good-byes, the fish
floating belliedup and bloated white,
pale as faces...

Wide-eyed, round as the world
the kids hang onto her words like onto her
in a high wind, hearing no old lady
reliving her past but lively Granny Noah
making ritual. When some rain falls
those remembrants make it their past, too;
a shower, a sprinkle, a tear
not likely to amount to much—

still, she hauls in the clothes. The kids help.
"It can't happen no more. God promised.
See that rainbow in the sky,
bright colors as these clothes
hung to dry—"
                    The kids have heard enough
They run out to play under the rainbow
easy on earth as animals. Granny watches
remembering her friend, imagining their grandchildren
playing with hers, her vision blurs.

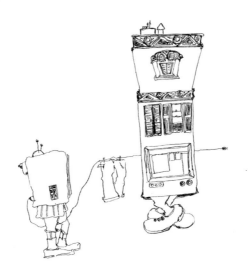

SLOWMOVING

Only her wrinkles run
and those all over each other
holding her hurt inside

out in the cold
comfortless, confused

she no longer tries to hide
she doesn't know
there's nothing left

to show.

LIMITS ARE TO LEAN ON,
LIKE FRIENDS

or family, familiar as the view
beyond the outer edge
walls hold the roof up, frame doors and windows
offer shelter against the wind

breakwaters, snowfences
sandbarriers: lines
shape space
lettering the spirit.

PROVENDER

Like a chipmunk
old Missus Berkowitz burrows.
Bit by bit, her barrow
looks and feels like home
making a bed of potato sacks
stuffed with magazines her doctor's office discarded,
twists of thread, rags and patches
minutes of meetings, posters, programs
and an ecumenical collection of church calendars
representing Greek, Roman and Jewish years
shredded for softness, squeezed small;
time, like space, is what Missus Berkowitz makes of it
remembering what she can and forgetting the rest
she lies down. Over the years
she's gotten used to not getting any younger
but being as old as she feels
she finds it's her feelings hurt
when the wind changes and the weather acts up
the dry skin cracks like bones
aching, or hearts
breaking
old ties, old habits
die hard. So she takes it easy
doing her best
no longer noticing there's nobody to tell her

       it isn't good enough.

PLAIN WOMAN

Even in her best
was not

dressy.

One used to take straight seams
and tidy hems for granted
but now they say
a lot. (*She* still wears skirts

and *stockings* to church.
To *church!*) Her own poetry
was against her: simple, direct
forthright as an old friend

she gave up waitressing
when her knees went.
It was never the money she missed

just the work.
Despite burning veins
and knobbled joints

she went on writing
till the end, so it wasn't over

even then.

O ADMIRABLE
ALL GNARLED SHAPES OF AGE

Olives
bent by centuries of bearing

pines
twisted rootward, leaning against the wind

bonsai
worked by hands patient as weather

woman
espalier'd against her bedboard

worn
outwait.

NATURAL

Down to earth, man
made small towns trudge
country roads.

THE WAY

roads are cutting up the countryside
soon there won't be any left. Surrounded by city
land gives way to names and numbers
addressing the wilderness
settlers spread out, stake claims to elbow room.
Now loneliness is not so far away.
We huddle: aliens, immigrants
trying to talk without a language in common
ground downtown, pushing and shoving
our children build Babel, block by block.
Then knock their own towers down—instant ruins
rubble. No threat to heaven; these days
nothing is built to last.
The kids go their separate ways, pedalling furiously
recycling space, leaving the land open
still as it ever was. We elders stretch out
in the golden silence, the sun shines. Peace and—
The country was never this quiet.
Insects skirled, birds shrilled warnings
wildbeasts snorted and snarled
screamed in triumph, tearing each other apart...

ALIENS IN THEIR OWN LAND

Exiled, resettled by decree
companies of kindred swarmed towards home
commanded by Caesar's census.
The great tradeways were crowded with prodigals
and dispossessed humbled to dust
returning, returning, they celebrated:
candles shone like little stars
and if one shone more brightly, who'd know?
Who'd know? Who'd heed the message
in the afterglow.

A SMALL TOWN CELEBRATES

its country Christmas
where parking lots are edged with fields
from whence they came
the stubbled and unshaven ground
underfoot as rough as potholed asphalt
and as gray

nearby trees quiver under an icy glitter
as bold squirrels play, leaping from stumps
to branches rejoicing in this season
of nuts and gatherings

shoppers scurry in and out of stores
packaged like the goods they carry
darting, chipper and alert
they have planned ahead and squirrelled away
furry and instinctive as the real natives
but with so much more left to do

Christmas is never far away.
Stables and mangers are part of the landscape,
sheep are scattered in the hillsides;
if shepherds are scarce, wise men in short supply
and it's hard to tell stars from satellites
still, something

lights up the sky.

IN THE NEIGHBORHOOD

English is always the second language
no matter what the first. Guttural squawks
burst into the suburbs as slogans
making room for new words, new sounds
saying something in what seems like secret codes.
Grunts and snarls, unambiguous snorts
growls and rapacious humming purrs
fill the air, making everything clear
heavy equipment rumbles into the neighborhood
roaring and bellowing: Make room! Make room!
Shoved over, the earth moves.

KEEPING UP with the TURN of the EARTH

the Joneses and other nomads, neighbors pioneer
clear the wilderness of rubbish
crowding their own kind
out in the wild

life thrives: bugs, birds, beasts
ethnics, gays, singles — barred
caged, kept (like women) in the zoo.
Species: endangered

survives, called names Adam never knew, but Eve — !
Eve heard the neighbors hissing
snaking through the grass
uprooted in her own backyard

she recycled that wasteland, naming no names
but places called home
making do, she spread the word
taming the wild, wide-open spaces.

– V –

from

IN MY BACKYARD

RESERVED FOR THE HANDICAPPED

The spaces are all filled
under the sign of the schematic wheelchair.
It must be Disability Day at the shopping center.

The driver of the green convertible
peels off, without looking
>   where she is going.
>   Blind?

>   A man comes out of the furniture
>   store
>   carrying his bed. Just healed
>   he hops into his van and hurries
>   away.
>   Who cured you? I call
>   but he doesn't hear.
>   Deaf.

Three kids and their sixpacks
clamber into a pickup
and roar off, opening fliptops
with their teeth.
Dumb?

Now the reserved spaces are empty.
There's room for the real disabilities:
self-pity, self-righteousness,
self-indulgence...

DEUS EX MACHINA

Making the world go
round, smoothing the rough edges
real people turn corners
as on a lathe. Spindleshanked beasts,
burdened, trudge the treadmill;
turning and returning, the stone grinds
slowly, ever so slowly
as God. As divinity descends
a spectacular, circular staircase
in stately, imperturbable revolutions
as cultures steal quietly down;
as vultures stoop, swoop
reel. God made the earth turn
but man invented the wheel.

HOW SHALL IT BE KNOWN,
WHAT IS PIPED OR HARPED?

The best minds of my generation are bi-lingual
speaking in tongues, wagging like tales
told by the dispossessed
determined to be understood. Petitioners stand
corrected, papers in hand; hot, sweaty, smudged
between the lines, perspective vanishes
making the point:
the primal scream is an anachronism—
English is not even a second language—
jargon is archaic—words an affectation—
acronyms are in. Abbreviating the spirit
deadly letters litter the landscape.
Decoders clutter the marketsquares,
each hawking her specialty, or his expertise:
taxes, insurance, social equity, education,
health, technology, development, government,
the arts, wills and compensation, property
rites of passage going places by getting by.
Talking a good line,
translators ease idioms out of the vernacular—
ah, who dares say what they mean?

Only the survivors of a select course of study,
followers of the prescribed curriculum past poetry,
philology, aesthetics, psycho-history, sociograms,
docudramas and diet manuals
to the purest of the pure:
                              forms
spare, ascetic
unfilled by anything but arcane directions.

After this basic training
the imaginative have been weeded out,
the knowledgeable disinspired,
the conscientious retired early,
leaving only a few chosen specialists
doomed to interpret
one branch of the bureaucracy to another.

THIS MISSION, HAS IT ACCOMPLISHED MUCH?

When our computers couldn't communicate
we tried talking directly
relied on the language we had in common,
sensing good and willing it to work
we identified ourselves.
They understood enough to ask
if we were the intelligent life on earth.
We laughed. Amused
               they told us about themselves

               their circling world
                 like ours, their sun
                   and stars, their moon
                     where men have been
and back. A complex people
with simple needs: food, clothing,
art. Their machines make everything
including war. Torn by doubts,
they've processed information
reduced thought to data, words to meaning
less than they say.

It all sounded so familiar!
Were we talking to ourselves?
Even if they weren't
what they said, it was wonderful:
not that they were like us
but that they liked us
instead.

THE FIRST THING I EVER READ

A cleanser label, the chick
new-hatched besides its egg
scrambling the text:
                    it hasn't scratched yet.
I knew that meant more than it said
but since my *bon ami* spoke some other language
we couldn't say much
and I early learned to let the picture talk.

Without words
writing is so much easier to understand.

SPECTATOR SPORTS

Watching people watching: the national past-time.
Nostalgia revives fellowcitizenry;
fans look back, across field
diamond, court. Recognizing each other
as in a dream, they cheer
jeer, hoot and holler.
No nation of strangers could speak
such a common language.
Surely home is a team if nothing else.

THE LIMNER

Anon, she painted so slowly
by slowly numbering her days.
Squares, color-full: a village green,
a town red; a sky
blue, heaven, shown with a gold star
shining through the cloudy silver
lining roads along a sunny yellow
corny field. Counting
houses, temples, schools, libraries,
gas stations, jails, shopping centers
she opened the world with windows
illuminating days of undated advent
in a calendar of continual, recorded praise.

SONG FOR A SOUL, SEARCHING

dumb animal
self, seeking
somebody

when I call
you, come.

PAGE FROM A COLORING BOOK

In all her pride and longing Spring
shivers in thin flowered slippers
watching herself, fixed in the frozen current
staring at the still stream while chill winds blow
across the edge of the mountain, and clouds slide
down the other side, uncovering a faint gold moon
thawing a blue pasteboard
all too early
afternoon.

BARTLETT'S FAMILIAR

This most companionable of all quotes:
the little lame echo, left after the piper
left bleating, calling
repeating the end of each phrase endlessly
so there is no end.

SUMMERS, SMALL CHILDREN

Shimmered at play, pretending
to be ready for bed while the light was still outside
and the soft talking of secrets slipped upstairs
through open windows. Wide awake,
when night was asleep inside
children crept quietly downstairs, in the dark
before day was light enough to see by.
Hours were glass then, weeks brass and shiny
as gold, molten into a month of Sundays.

We grew old as children
telling each other stories Time told.
What good was all we cracked it up to be?
Between first and second childhoods, the middle
aged like a fine wine, or cheese
saved for a special occasion, celebrating
the myths and legends of a lifetime, forever
young enough to look forward to looking back.

NOT AS A DREAM

I was awakened suddenly by the middle of night
shaking her hairy scales; scared
into the midst of living daylights
I knew what she knew, the dark old bruise:

Man's dominion over all that lives
leaves death unmastered. Ennobling pain
sanctifies, and hurts. There's a dry ache lingers
after grief, like a killer who can't, quite—

Creation's cruel, despite love and beauty.
What kind, or kind of, God accounts sufferings good?
And if these are not His doings, whose?

LAMENT FOR A DEAD MESSENGER

Mourn, withdraw, repent. Smash the TV.
Burn the papers, throw the radio out the window—
turn the mirror to the wall.

Remembering times of simple good
old days live again, night after comfortable night.
News doesn't happen—just daily events
re-enacted around the fire
light dawns. Grays shadow the known world;
the unknown disappears
like smoke. Only reality is left.
Crime, sex and violence are commonplace;
the ordinary is everyday. Nothing is sacred,
simply rated PG. When the parents I knew grew up,
silent as movies, seen and not heard,
secrets were kept. And promises.
Now privacy is invaded, like a rich country.
The defenseless are ravaged,
unburied dead litter the landscape,
biodegraded. All waste is hazardous.

The endless war to end wars continues:
history is rerun for want of something more exciting.
Commercial messages provide welcome interruptions;
public service pronouncements berate private enterprise.
Speech is free, talk is cheap, time costs.
Self-confessed murderers interview each other,
advocating permanent abolition of the death penalty
with automatic parole for the best possible behavior
under the circumstances. The rest of us demand equal time,
served as victims and other endangered species
sentenced to real life—

Smash the TV.
Burn the papers; throw the radio out the window.

Turn the mirror to the wall.

SCHOOL

This world is no less real for seeming small
and self-contained. Numbering no natives,
citizens, wayfarers are welcomed
as perfect strangers become imperfect
friends. Everyone has come from somewhere
is going somewhere, or wishes (at least sometime)
to be somewhere else. Dreams and memories
those farthest of all horizons
extend this world through walls of windows
seen through darkly: glass
in all its storied glory
stained.

– VI –

from

THE EVENING AND THE MORNING OF THE SAME DAY

BEDLAM

The decree has gone forth.
For reasons of health, even homeless
humans can't sleep in stables
like beasts. Counted among men
crowded into a crazy world, frightened
hungry and cold in the cruel—it's unnatural!
Even animals wouldn't live like that
but people have their rights
if not much else.
                                Poor shabbies,
swathed in their woolly bests
unravel like sweaters, snag on any sudden snatch
or jerk of the heartstrings. They smell
what the wind blows: home. Cooking or fires
placed on the street, cornered
shadow and substance slide, as on ice.
Reflections stumble and fall all to pieces
breaking not themselves but the mirror.
Crouching on the edge of reality—
asylum is everywhere. The whole place is a madhouse.
The decree has gone forth.

COME CHRISTMAS

We can all be kings
bearing acceptable gifts
for once, each choice the right one
be it something or self
we living sacrifices give, as children do
what we'd like to get

sure that a baby in a manger
needs absolutely everything.

PEACE MARCH ON PALM SUNDAY

Banners balloon, brightening the almost warm
early spring sunshine. Hopes stand around
in little groups, whistling, waving,
waiting to join the parade. Underfoot
dumpy harbingers of nonviolence coup and murmur softly
as pigeons do. Hawks vend: hot underdogs, sodapopcorn.
Native and honorable, profits inspire the crowd.
Almost unnoticed, the parade starts
slowly, so everyone can keep up and enjoy
bearing witness like palms. Springs green and shade;
the Sunday breeze blows; no bands drown
amiable chatter (oh, how peace talks!)
as the march meanders. The police are friendly;
fellowcitizenship beams and glistens; smiles glow
golden and toothy. (Grins gaped in dead mouths
speaking of peace in that sometime
so long ago, once—) Upon a predetermined route,
headlights blink in broad daylight,
pale as faces reflected in windows
watching peace amble by.

The drummer's far too distant to set the beat.
Noonday heat shimmers; spectators clap and chant,
cheer stragglers on. Underfoot like pigeons
doves scuff and murmur, pecking the order (open beaked,
shouting, stirring the crowd): "Give me an H!
Give me an O! HO-sanna! HO- sanna!

Ho, ho, ho-chi-minh! Ho, ho!
Hey, hey, LBJ! How many kids did you kill today?"
Kids, undead and led by betters old enough to know,
stamp and bellow: "Left, right!
Left, right! Make war on the military!
Fight, fight, fight!" Ignorant armies march
by day as well as night. The steady thump of feet
dulls souls; stamping, tramping,
walking all over the world, each other and anybody
who can't keep up or get out of the way—
"Hey! It's nothing personal!"
The mob moves forward.

Something snaps.
Gunshot? Backfire? Balloon popping? Stunned,
hot and sweaty, violence strikes
and nonviolence strikes back.
Swarming across the barricade,
barbarians on both sides cry (oh, how war cries!):
"Crucify Him! Crucify Him! Crucify—"
                                        Parade rest.

The law has been laid down, like life
or arms; hands, washed, hang empty
holding nothing, not even their own.
Crowds drift and fade.
Perhaps peace is not something that can be made.

IN THE LEAST RESTRICTIVE ENVIRONMENT

everything comes hard to him
even the easiest. Walking, talking
feeling his ways
hurt, he stumble. Fall
foaming; spitting, stutters
a syllable at a time.
Spasms catch him, stiff, crookit.
How he looked, he never remembers
so they tell him:
spastic, dummy
retard. Like a little children
he learns slowly
he's best at something:
suffering. So he hangs onto it,
another cross
he can't bear.

MUGGING VICTIM

Battered (as a child) old body
slumps, blinks. The little
wrinkled hands fold, prayerful
(as in peace). Who'd have thought
there'd be anything to hold
so tight (as sleep)? Murmuring,
friends coo. Comfort's dovelike,
lulling; worried angels wing and buck
the passing but man don't live
by bread alone. Like pigeons do.

WHAT BUT THE WORLD WILL BE
TORN APART?

Children who fend for themselves
survive against all odds
even their own kind.
Eaten out of house and home
as from a trap, they get away
leaving parts of themselves behind
they run for their lives
like animals, wild
but not free, they play
gathering whatever earth scatters
at their feet. Their ways hers
they hunt; others prey.

I HADN'T EXPECTED
STARS THIS MORNING

but a little patch of local wonder
shone
neighboring as lighted windows, day
dreamed in other people's houses;
sunshine filled mine. Dust sparkled,
motes beamed:
reality was what it seemed.

LIGHT

Early as morning
lying lightly along the window
framing day
trying to come in
out of the cold.

CAN ANYTHING SO BLACK

be considered clear? Although
this night's sky will thin
and pale towards morning
now not even the edges show
along what would be an horizon
heaven's a mere shadow on the snow.

THE SUN IS A SHINY DAY

and a dark night.
Between them, the difference

lies. Truth hurts.
Wounds heal while telling time
it's worse than pain

not to feel.

JARGON SPOKEN HERE

Fluent facilitators interface with multi-lingual peers,
translating deeds into words with all deliberate
speed. (Caution: DON'T. Conviction
means loss of license.) Deregulated
inequities persist; the developmentally disenfranchised
resist class actions, in and out of school. (Caution: Slow
Children at Play). Reverbalized, discriminations
are more easily dismissed. (Caution: Men
Working). Once the differences were clear
without a sign. Now...well, on paper
the world is a better place
but for anything over two dimensions
difficult to live in.

MRS. R.W.

Losing home, family and fortune
led to a job holding my own
until I was let go
when I lost control of everything
including my bladder.
Committed to custodial care
I kept track of simple things:
sights, smells, sounds.
Then my senses left me
just what I could remember
forgetting: myself.

TEACHER

lived near school
next door to neighbors
with her Books and Papers
and Cat
coming in through the open window.
Flowerpatching her salad garden,
shaking her shade tree, raking the leaves
left behind, she was not nearly so lonesome
as she seemed. Working long hours
she kept busy all day, and all night
she dreamed.

PILGRIM

born far from here
he died among such good friends
as seen bereft without him.
Buried in his adopted land
he took root; grew
native as grief
greening the cold ground.

FARM HANDS

Theys worn, smooth
the hide hardened
thick as leather. Dried, tanned,
worked, weather or not
in and out of pocket they hold
body and soul together.

GWYNETTE

Here, old lovey—
shawl be it.
The paisley pride this pm,
Fur's evening,
something to slink into,
soft as night.
Morning is a fuzzy time,
woollen and shedding,
cuddly. But now
between noon and nightfall
a little color cramps the chill.
Pinch the pale cheeks,
bite the lips red,
ring the fingers.
Swathe bones in what becomes them
best, besides a little rest.

I CRY FOR OTHER THINGS
THAN DEATH

parades, Christmas
trees and Easter trumpets (rising
on a bright spring day
to tears' occasion, clean
as rain); toothaches, splinters,
scraped knees (the sting
and itch of healing
humbles pain); dog's comfort;
an unexpected present, perfect
for some rare, unspecial day;
dreams (come true
when all that's real
won't come again). I cry
for simple things, for all
I bear for you no longer
here to share.

SUNDAY PAINTERS

splatter the grass;
smocked and crimped
the smooth green
flowers. Wormed
colors pale,
soften in the sun
strokes. Brushed
easy among easels,
painters stretch,
lay back, admiring
the view: just beyond
the horizon, clouds
castle and sky
lines meet, point
and vanish. The sun
sets. Godly, even
perspective rests.

FRIEND BODY

Faithful animal self
trusting and loyal as a dog
leaps, plays, delights in food
and sleep and praise,
curls tight against the cold,
guards works and days, strays near
in journeys far from here.

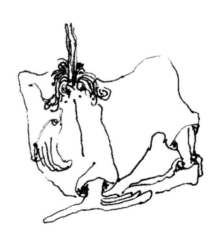

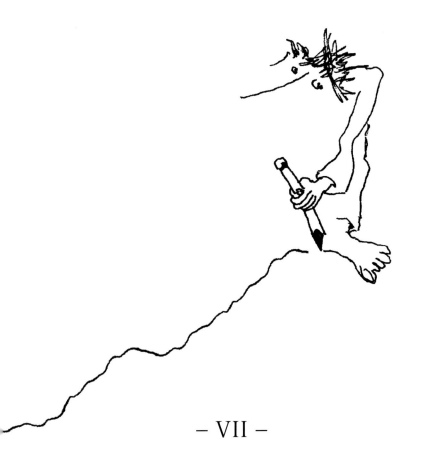

– VII –

FRAGMENTS

IN THE BEGINNING

Was the word
          from our sponsor.

BOOKS

   Boxed words.
Footnotes on snow
          white pages.

LIGHT

   Snow falling
harder and harder
               heavy
                    white.

I LIKE BOOK JACKETS

old comfortable clothes, soft sheets
protective coloring, skin on bones
landscapes with houses, roads into the distance
ships at sea—the human touch
stones marking graves.

DEAD AS LANGUAGE

original as sin
virtual as reality—
       themes doublepark
    traffic lights the dark.

STILL

pictures, last scene:
earthen sky, line cast
a shadow of light
waves sound good-bye.

RINSE WATER

colors run
dry

Washed rainbows
lie between tide and turning
one element into another.

AFTER THE IMAGE

Reality surfaces, swims into focus.
Fished out of water, airs
upon the common ground

watered down, or fired up
elemental: sound.

MARGINAL AS EXISTENCE

Amphibians skim surfaces
surviving what one element does to another
reality evolves along the edges,
in suburban sprawls nomadic hunters gather,
settle in abandoned malls.

ARTIFACT

Jars
preconceptions: solid, dimensional
an object, labelled "pen"
ultimate sword or plowshare
archetypical relic of the post-historic era
ours.

VIRTUAL VERNACULAR

In the landscape of exile
language is home
made welcome

> living hand-to-mouth
> eating words.

FOR US THERE ARE NO SEASONS

Climate controlled, the global village
unweathers storms, warms, cools
a constant temperate calm
twilight dawns: not quite dark enough
for shadows, nor light enough to read by

sea. Inland at low tide
savourless salt of the earth dries
encrusts the edge of the world, rimy rim
grimy plastic pools
spill chemically treated liquid
distill waters
dampen the land's dusts.

WHAT'S REAL

Estate taxes the imagination:
cut down to size, or blown
out of proportion
covered up, scaled down
mountain or molehill—
a place in the wilderness
or developable space
with a view: Home grown
                    over
                look:
          My backyard's greener
              pastures mown.

LENTEN CALENDAR

                    Little windows of denial
              thresholds of pain, doubt, desire
                    opening to interpretation

                          let the easy way out
                    like a little household pet
                groomed, fed, too well-bred
                    to survive the wilderness

              once off the beaten track, intrigued
              beyond temptation to turn back.

BIRD ON A BARE BRANCH

Brown leaf
dries, falls
    an old lady
        too cold to be hungry
            lies still
                about her age.

DNR

Courage, old lady
skating on thin ice
    graceful, gallant
        hero happened along

Time ran out, slipping, sliding
sank below the surface
            of those still waters
                cold, deep
                    drowned

not fast, nor yet asleep
        in a coma, unable to refuse
            heroic measures
lose what heroes choose.

TIME TAKES TOO LONG

Healing, slow as spring the hurts of winter
warm what cold comfort aches;
restored to feeling, breaks and stings
un-numbered, pains welcomed—
Old friend, no end to suffering.

THE DEAD OF WINTER

Cold comforts still
'til the dead of spring
green, quicken; will the dead of summer
thrive, thicken? ripen, fall
the dead of harvest
nourish all.

PULLING TIDES IN AND OUT

along the shoreline
drawing water
colors dry
wash out.

DICTIONARY

Definition: A poem

words with strings attached
hung out on a line.

SOW FIELDS; GREEN YIELDS GROW

white to harvest, blow dandelion
gone to seed: milkweed
light as snow.

BEEN LOST ALL LENT

Between Emmaus and Damascus
commuters, trafficking in sprawl,
crawl behind nomads and refugees
pilgrims lined up to find themselves
in the wilderness within.

THE NATIVES LEFT

Nothing behind but tourists
trapped barbarians, posed
pictured as perfect on postcards
sold at the gates.

SUBURBAN RENAISSANCE

Real lives lived here:
transient consumers at the mall
nomadic commuters at the bazaar
a majority of ethnics make minority rites
    true tests of tribal awareness
as bargain hunters gather
growing economies in the wilderness
indigenous loyalties, pledged to a common
    heritage: brand names.

PEOPLED HILLS

Parsed valleys, vernacular landscapes
settled in their ways
mean the end is just

over the horizon;
lined with family trees
rerouted along the information highway

keeping noise, dust and traffic
out of everybody's backyards.

POEM PUT HER FEET ON

Bones and skin went walkabout
the wilderness within

unstill, life unrolls
scrolls: treadmills
grinding the words
slowly
        gathering
                speed

Limits exercise imagination
bodies of work
play; act: pretend.

Take parts of speech;
flesh out the soul, vernacular
indigenous, and whole.

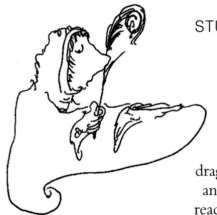

STUMBLE INTO EDEN

After the fall
it takes all winter
'til spring
arrives; survives
unseasonable cold
snap
dragons roar, bees bumble
and before long: summer
reading lists, and weeding.

ALL LENT LONG

Winter lingers into spring
longer and longer these days
the light stays later
leaving shadows behind
gentle old friends
keep cold out
in what's left of the dark.

BETWEEN LINES WRITTEN IN SPRING

Wintering over. Sun
light without heat

cold, hard facts of life
thaw, melt, flood

waters unearth
mud.

DRAWING NIGH

the horizon; lines drawn
details emerge
out of the background
such subtle shades of meaning
as perspective fades
everything comes close enough
to touch.

LOOKING AT THE BIG PICTURE

So full of little things
details, squeezed for space
slide into the margins: spotlight
life on the edge illuminates
the very brink of existence.

WAITING IS A KIND OF SPRING

Not into action, a break
in habit, kept coiled
already leapt at, the change
taken.

THAT OLD BARBARIAN, SPRING

At the gates, the dooryards
crack the pavements
unflowering wild
green grows back.

DAYLIGHT DOESN'T SAVE TIME

even from the dark; shadows
stretched out in the sun
burn, blacken: night
done to a turn.

TV COVERAGE OF
MILLENNIAL CELEBRATIONS

Midnight everlasting
evenings of the morning
all in the same day
breaking news:

All the kingdom of the world
in a moment of time
tuned in to eternity
just for a split second

chance.

PRAYERS AND COMMERCIALS

Having so much to answer for, language
speaks for itself
              abused
         in the marketplace
    as children, old before their time
              pipe and dance
sing: warnings
  bought and sold
    for a second chance.

RETURNING WITH THE SPRING

Uncleaning ladies
bagged like groceries
unseasonable tourists
trapped between global warming
(regulatory jungle rot
proliferating jargon) and the new ice age
(cold, implacable forms
predatory bureaucrats sunk in hibernation)
survive daily living
dangerously.

PICTURE WINDOWS
ON ALBUM STREET

Quiet old night sky
light looking around
turns black corners

Back; holds still
life fades:
mellow shadows
yellow shades.

HUNCHED AND BUNDLED

out in the cold
like cartoon characters
we catch our breath, taken away
watch death burst the bubble
leaving us nothing to say.

PEOPLE IN THEIR POEMS

wear words out
in the open.

STORIES ARE TO TELL

the truth
  lies still: small voice
    silent reading
      allowed.

LEARNED BY HEART

Broken
english only
spoken in translation
token gesture, a sign
language
barrier crossed like a palm, reader
money talks
telling time truth is not the whole story,
words without pictures unpeople a landscape
the mother tongue describes
fatherland
children call collect.

PROTOTYPICAL

Primitive life forms
in the margins of existence,
edged out of Eden, exiled

evolving as a common language
translating deed into word
fleshed out, animate

survivors of an unimaginable reality.

PREHISTORY

Repeats itself without commercial interruptions
sponsorless news
                    makers, movers and shakers
hunters gather, bargaining
                    betting, trading

Places: mysterious and sacred, wild
  animal instincts, natural as disasters
                    droughts, floods—
  earth suns herself, burns

Learns. Buy experience:
                         passionate consumers
                              devour returns.

SKETCHES FROM
AN IMAGINARY JOURNAL

Drawn on real life:
is nature human
                    being out of one element
          made into another?

OUTSIDE THE LINES

Colors run
errands of mercy, killing
time in space
filling the background with music:
A perspective not only seen
but smelt, heard, held, felt.

WORDS REST

tired of playing around
quiet down; whisper to each other
or read themselves
sound asleep.

LIGHT STRIPPED THE DARK NAKED

vulnerable shadows shone, stark
against the bright known.

DISTANCE

Disappears in the light
snow, falling
angels.

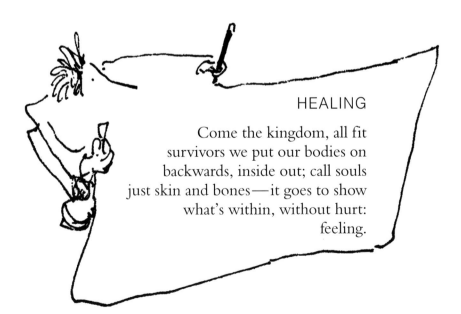

HEALING

Come the kingdom, all fit
survivors we put our bodies on
backwards, inside out; call souls
just skin and bones—it goes to show
what's within, without hurt:
feeling.

LEAP! SPRING

off and away
behind her muddy footprints
follow
our feet of clay.

STREETS AT THE END OF WINTER

turn towards spring; cornered
the village greens.

POET OF THIS PARISH

Homes in, plain pigeon
english broken here
in her own backyard
lumpy little local muse
translates between the lines
drawn to daily living
language her ark, dove leaves
her mark.

spirit, steadied by the flesh
readied, willing
eager even to die, and go—

to heaven? why leave
the little corner garden
the room with books
the coffee shop—
            dearly loved
humans and other beings, met again
leaven eternity with life
saving graces: familiar faces—

but places! oh
so hard to say goodbye.

I CALL ON POETS, FRIENDS

come calling, words in hand
visiting books
civil, sometimes, or sad; furious
meddling, peddling wares; crazed
weary, mad with joy
dazed, amazed—
as lonely in my company
        as I in theirs.

FEELING IS ALWAYS BETTER

even when it hurts,
healing.

TIME IS TAKING ITS TIME THESE DAYS

going no place fast
moving at such an easy pace
even I can keep up.

IN THE COLD HOUR
JUST BEFORE DAWN, DARK
UNFOLDS HER STARRY BLANKET
AND PUTS IT ON

WORDS

Say what we mean:
name, bless — wordless
world were wilderness.

AFTERWORDS, ACKNOWLEDGEMENTS

I WAS READ TO GENEROUSLY as a child. The worlds of Pooh, Piglet and Christopher Robin, Ratty and Mole, and Mary Poppins were as real to me as my own. I learned to read with Dick and Jane—now maligned, those primers seemed to me just another story. Leaving the theatre after Peter Pan, I saw thousands of Tinkerbelles, reflected from windows, wires—stars lit Broadway. By the time my family got TV, I was still young enough to suspend disbelief. Burr Tillstrom coming onstage with Kukla, Fran, and Ollie may have ended each program but began my search for the real reality, backstage.

My first encounter with words and pictures meaning more than they seemed was struggling to decipher the relationship between slogan and logos on the Bon Ami cleanser can. Intimations of the power of the image led to a fascination with advertisement, and poetry. After a Vassar College experimental theatre production of *The Mother of Us All,* as my Aunt Mabel explained what Stein and Thomson were trying to do, I began to wonder if meaning—as commonly understood—might not be all that mattered.

Wonderful teachers at the Arlington Grade School, Emma Willard School, and Vassar College bore with the twists and turns of my learning curves. The beginning of wisdom is so often beginning again. Colleagues: fellow students, actors and technicians, teachers, booksellers and buyers, librarians, board members, volunteers—we may have worked on things other than this book, but all that work has gone into it. A kind and caring medical community, particularly at Northern Dutchess Hospital, keeps me going, as do a legion of good friends who offer support even when I don't ask. Jamie and Barney Baxter, Trudy Hanmer, and M.S. Mangat, MD have made more difference than they could imagine.

By publishing early work, *The Barrytown Explorer, Art Scene, The Christian Century* and *The National Review* encouraged me when this book wasn't even a dream. Merritt Donaghy Betts has read, and reread, acres of works-in-progress with enthusiasm, perception and unwavering generosity of spirit. She, Pat and Sven Peterson, Edith Prescott, Jerry Gallagher, Debbie Stone, and Dona McLaughlin gave impetus and encouragement to earlier drafts. The Starr Library has been steadfast in providing resources, including Joseph (Trip) Sinnott, who just happened to be there proofreading something else when I realized I, with a book in search of a publisher, just might suspend disbelief once again. Trip's perspective and guidance, compounded by kindness, confidence, humor and good sense (including a technological component) maintains the great tradition of editorial friendship. The staff of College Avenue Press has been wonderful.

My family is a widespread sheltering tree, from which I can see the forest…which quite literally makes this book possible. And, when I get cumbered about with this or other projects, my sister Tuna shows me that everything comes out in the wash.

DRIPPING DRYWASH

There is no way to really thank everybody who helped this book happen, except to say "Thank you," trusting one and all to read between the lines.

– KATH

LIKE LITTLE LOST FRIENDS

words wander
far from home
making up a story
telling childhood's imaginary companion
anything to help
adults pretend to grow up.

KATH HOWELL
A SELF-PORTRAIT

*B*ORN IN Poughkeepsie, NY, I grew up in what was then rural Dutchess County. I attended local public schools through ninth grade, until I became a boarder at the Emma Willard School in Troy, NY, graduating in 1958. I entered Vassar College that fall, withdrew and was hospitalized for treatment for a nervous breakdown. I reentered Vassar and graduated in 1964. Graduate work at the University of Minnesota fell short of a degree but included the 1964-65 season at the Tyrone Guthrie Theater, as a McKnight Fellow in Playwriting.

Thus formally educated, I compiled a chequered résumé of gainful and ungainful employment, including a stint as buyer at the Vassar Cooperative Bookshop, teaching at Emma Willard, volunteering with the Vassar Office of Off-Campus Studies, at Emma Willard, local schools, and the Northern Dutchess Hospital.

I've had the chance to travel in Europe and Africa, and live on a Caribbean Island. Vassar Experimental Theater, Tyrone

Guthrie Theater, Emma Willard School and the Rensselaer County Community players let me work in and write for their stages.

I started to draw "seriously" during a season of political involvement—doodles eventually developed into cartoon minutes of meetings, comments on life and times. I have on occasion dreamed my characters were drawing me. Since the poems are drawn from real lives—some of them mine—some context is in order: Despite preferring hands-on responsibility, I've found service on boards and committees—even fundraising—surprisingly satisfying. Brought up a Methodist, I'm now at home in the Episcopal tradition...although I still miss certain rousing if politically incorrect hymns. I've been hospitalized off and on for myasthenia gravis—it's a chronic disease and we're learning to live with each other, helped by firm and friendly medical assistance.

I gave up the Dodgers when they gave up Brooklyn, but the Red Sox keep me waiting for next year. I have an away from homebase in Marion, MA, but live mostly in Rhinebeck, NY, not far from where I began.

BRUSH WITH REALITY IS A collection of poems and drawings about ordinary wonders and extraordinary routines. The delights of daily living are celebrated. The doubts of the faithful honored. The fearful hopes that make our world go round affirmed. Between the lines of words and pictures, hopeful fears are acknowledged, black and white sometimes relieved in color.

The poems in this collection were written (and rewritten) between 1962 and 2002. They arose from the poet's concerns with prevailing currents in America during those years: rural and urban sprawling toward suburbia; the inclusion of TV as neighbor as well as icon; the image as advertised, graven or not. References to theater, art, the Middle Ages and the Bible are the common ground—the public space—for personal events: growing up, and old; going to school, to war, to work. The drawings and paintings illustrate the challenge to perspective of these juxtapositions.